A Three 16 Christmas

by

Shelley Spiers

A Three 16 Christmas

Printed in the UK

ISBN: 978-1-62020-108-4

AMBASSADOR INTERNATIONAL
Emerald House
427 Wade Hampton Blvd.
Greenville, SC 29609, USA
www.ambassador-international.com

AMBASSADOR BOOKS
The Mount
2 Woodstock Link
Belfast, BT6 8DD, Northern Ireland, UK
www.ambassador-international.com

The colophon is a trademark of Ambassador

by

Shelley Spiers

AMBASSADOR INTERNATIONAL

GREENVILLE, SOUTH CAROLINA & BELFAST, NORTHERN IRELAND

www.ambassador-international.com

NOTE:

some passages in this booklet are taken directly from the Bible. These will be indented and in italics.

Introduction

I wonder what you think of when you hear the word Christmas?

Maybe you think of enjoying a break from work and spending time with family and friends? Perhaps you think of the excitement of finding that perfect gift for someone special and your anticipation as you await their reaction on Christmas morning?

Many other things could come to mind: the fairy lights that never work on the first try (even though they were in perfect working order when you packed them away); the manic scenes in supermarkets across the country as shoppers buy enough to feed an army for a month, even though they're only cooking for three and the shops will be open again in 48 hours or less; or the challenge that faces households everywhere – 'How many creative dishes can we produce in the week following Christmas that will make use of all the leftover turkey?'

How about a teenage girl giving birth in a dusty stable; being visited by humble shepherds and strangers from a faraway land, and later having to flee to a foreign country to escape from an evil king who wanted to harm the child? This is probably not what comes to mind when you hear the word 'Christmas'. But this event is central to the true meaning of Christmas. It was part of a very special plan that has eternal significance for you and me.

The title of this booklet is 'A Three16 Christmas'. In the Bible, in John chapter 3 and verse 16, we read:

> *'For God so loved the world that he gave his one and only Son, that whoever believes in him shall not perish but have eternal life.'*

Read on to discover how this verse defines the true meaning of Christmas; and how Christmas is not an end in itself but rather the beginning of a very special plan: A plan that was set in place especially for YOU!

In the beginning there was God.

God is pure and holy.

He created the heavens and the earth.

He created all things – the sky; the seas; the sun, moon and stars; animals of the land, sky and sea; plants and trees.......

The list is endless!

He created people in his own image.

The first man and woman were called Adam and Eve. At first, they enjoyed a perfect relationship with God.

God gave them a beautiful garden to live in and to look after. He told them that they could eat from any tree in the garden except one tree, which was called the tree of the knowledge of good and evil. God said that if they ate from this tree, they would die.

God gave people free will: The ability to make decisions.

Adam and Eve chose to disobey God by eating from the forbidden tree and, as a consequence, sin entered the world.

Everyone born since Adam and Eve has been born with the problem of sin. Sin means rejecting God's rule over us and choosing to go our own way and not his; disobeying God in the wrong things that we think, say and do; and failing to do things that we should do.

This sin separates us from God and it means that we cannot go to heaven – God's perfect home.

God is a God of justice and therefore sin must be punished. The punishment for sin is death – separation from God forever in a place the Bible calls hell.

However, God is also a God of love.

He had a rescue plan……

John 1:1-5 and 14

"In the beginning was the Word, and the Word was with God, and the Word was God. He was with God in the beginning. Through him all things were made; without him nothing was made that has been made. In him was life, and that life was the light of men. The light shines in the darkness, but the darkness has not understood it."

"The Word became flesh and made his dwelling among us. We have seen his glory, the glory of the one and only, who came from the Father, full of grace and truth."

The Word

The Word;
The one through whom and by whom
all things were made.
The Word became flesh and lived among us.

The Word;
The one who spoke the earth into being,
who designed each uniquely intricate snowflake
and composed the sweet song of the nightingale.
The Word became flesh and lived among us.

The Word;
The one who flung stars into space,
who set the planets in orbit
and breathed life into mankind.
The Word became flesh and lived among us.

The Word;
The Son of God,
Light of the World;
Fully God, fully man;
Our Rescuer.
The Word became flesh and lived among us.

The Word;
To all who received him

he gave the right to be called
Children of God.
The Word became flesh and lived among us.

The Birth of Jesus Foretold (Luke 1:26-38)

In the sixth month, God sent the angel Gabriel to Nazareth, a town in Galilee, to a virgin pledged to be married to a man named Joseph, a descendant of David. The virgin's name was Mary. The angel went to her and said, "Greetings, you who are highly favoured! The Lord is with you."

Mary was greatly troubled at his words and wondered what kind of greeting this might be. But the angel said to her, "Do not be afraid, Mary; you have found favour with God. You will be with child and give birth to a son, and you are to give him the name Jesus. He will be great and will be called the Son of the Most High. The Lord God will give him the throne of his father David, and he will reign over the house of Jacob forever; his kingdom will never end."

"How will this be?" Mary asked the angel, "Since I am a virgin?"

The angel answered, "The Holy Spirit will come upon you, and the power of the Most High will overshadow you. So the holy one to be born will be called the Son of God. Even Elizabeth your relative is going to have a child in her old age, and she who was said to barren is in her sixth month. For nothing is impossible with God."

"I am the Lord's servant," Mary answered. "May it be to me as you have said." Then the angel left her.

Mary

Startled!
An angel appears
bringing news of a child.
A baby?
For me?
Surely it's impossible
for a virgin to conceive?

Terrified!
What about Joseph?
How to explain?
Imagine the scandal,
the stares and the shouts!
I'll surely be stoned
when the news gets out.

Amazed
by words of comfort,
of hope,
of joy.
The child that I carry
is a special baby boy.
A saviour,
sent from God!

Overjoyed
that the LORD
has blessed his servant.
The mighty one has done
great things.
May it be to me
just as you say!

I'm just a young girl
but Father,
I'm yours!

The Birth of Jesus Christ (Matthew 1:18-23)

This is how the birth of Jesus Christ came about: His mother Mary was pledged to be married to Joseph, but before they came together, she was found to be with child through the Holy Spirit.

Because Joseph her husband was a righteous man and did not want to expose her to public disgrace, he had in mind to divorce her quietly.

But after he had considered this, an angel of the Lord appeared to him in a dream and said, "Joseph son of David, do not be afraid to take Mary home as your wife, because what is conceived in her is from the Holy Spirit.

She will give birth to a son, and you are to give him the name Jesus, because he will save his people from their sins."

All this took place to fulfill what the Lord had said through the prophet:

"The virgin will be with child and will give birth to a son, and they will call him Immanuel— which means, God with us."

Joseph

Betrothed;
A love declared,
A future promised
to Mary,
my beloved.

But then
a shock;
a scandal.
A baby, not mine,
for Mary
my beloved.

A dilemma:
What could I do
but walk away
quietly
and spare the shame
and disgrace
of Mary
my beloved?

But then
in the night,
appeared an angel
with a message.

"Do not fear!
Marry Mary
your beloved."

A baby
sent from God.
A saviour,
Jesus.
God's chosen servant
is Mary
my beloved.

If God
is in it,
I cannot walk away.
It won't be easy
but it's exactly
where I want to be.

The Birth of Jesus (Luke 2: 1-7)

In those days Caesar Augustus issued a decree that a census should be taken of the entire Roman world. (This was the first census that took place while Quirinius was governor of Syria.) And everyone went to his own town to register.

So Joseph also went up from the town of Nazareth in Galilee, to Judea, to Bethlehem the town of David, because he belonged to the house and line of David. He went there to register with Mary, who was pledged to be married to him and was expecting a child.

While they were there, the time came for the baby to be born, and she gave birth to her firstborn, a son. She wrapped him in cloths and placed him in a manger, because there was no room for them in the inn.

The Shepherds and the Angels (Luke 2:8-20)

And there were shepherds living out in the fields nearby, keeping watch over their flocks at night.

An angel of the Lord appeared to them, and the glory of the Lord shone around them, and they were terrified.

But the angel said to them, "Do not be afraid. I bring you good news of great joy that will be for all the people.

Today in the town of David, a Saviour has been born to you; he is Christ the Lord.

This will be a sign to you: You will find a baby wrapped in cloths and lying in a manger."

Suddenly a great company of the heavenly host appeared with the angel, praising God and saying,

"Glory to God in the highest, and on earth peace to men on whom his favour rests."

When the angels had left them and gone into heaven, the shepherds said to one another, "Let's go to Bethlehem and see this thing that has happened, which the Lord has told us about."

So they hurried off and found Mary and Joseph, and the baby, who was lying in the manger.

When they had seen him, they spread the word concerning what had been told them about this child, and all who heard it were amazed at what the shepherds said to them. But Mary treasured up all these things and pondered them in her heart. The shepherds returned, glorifying and praising God for all the things they had heard and seen, which were just as they had been told.

There were Shepherds

There were shepherds on a hillside
Keeping watch before the dawn,
When a host of heaven's angels
Brought the news that Christ was born.
They found him in a manger
And on their knees they fell
As they worshipped the Messiah,
God with us,
Immanuel.

On their search for the Messiah
Travelled wise men from afar.
They were guided on their journey
By a bright and shining star.
In Bethlehem they found him
As the prophets had foretold
And they laid their gifts before him;
Myrrh, Frankincense and Gold.

Glory, glory in the highest;
Joy and peace to men on earth.
Join our song of jubilation
To celebrate the Saviour's birth.
May that star guide you to Jesus,
May you hear the angel song.
May the peace and joy of Christmas
Be in your heart the whole year long.

Visitors Arrive from Eastern Lands (Matthew 2:1-12)

After Jesus was born in Bethlehem in Judea, during the time of King Herod, Magi from the east came to Jerusalem and asked, "Where is the one who has been born king of the Jews? We saw his star in the east and have come to worship him." When King Herod heard this he was disturbed, and all Jerusalem with him. When he had called together all the people's chief priests and teachers of the law, he asked them where the Christ was to be born. "In Bethlehem in Judea," they replied, "for this is what the prophet has written:

"'But you, Bethlehem, in the land of Judah, are by no means least among the rulers of Judah; for out of you will come a ruler, who will be the shepherd of my people Israel."

Then Herod called the Magi secretly and found out from them the exact time the star had appeared. He sent them to Bethlehem and said, "Go and make a careful search for the child. As soon as you find him, report to me, so that I too may go and worship him."

After they had heard the king, they went on their way, and the star they had seen in the east went ahead of them until it stopped over the place where the child was. When they saw the star, they were overjoyed. On coming to the house, they saw the child with his mother Mary, and they bowed down and worshipped him. Then they opened their treasures and presented him with gifts of gold, and of incense and of myrrh. And having been warned in a dream not to go back to Herod, they returned to their country by another route.

Travelling

Travelling,
From lands afar,
In search of a newborn King.
Have you seen him?

Following,
A bright shining star,
In search of a newborn King.
Have you seen him?

Bringing gifts;
Bowing to worship
The newborn King.
We have seen him.

Bringing Gold,
A gift for a King.
Pure, refined gold
For a pure, spotless lamb.

Bringing Frankincense,
The scent of sweet smelling worship
For Immanuel
God with us.

Bringing Myrrh,
A bitter cup

For one who would
Suffer and die
For the sins of the world.

Returning,
Warned in a dream
To go back another way.

Changed,
Not only in the path we have chosen.
Having seen him,
We'll never be the same.

Have you seen him?

The Prophecy of Simeon (Luke 2:25-35)

Now there was a man in Jerusalem called Simeon, who was righteous and devout. He was waiting for the consolation of Israel, and the Holy Spirit was upon him. It had been revealed to him by the Holy Spirit that he would not die before he had seen the Lord's Christ. Moved by the Spirit, he went into the temple courts. When the parents brought in the child Jesus to do for him what the custom of the Law required, Simeon took him in his arms and praised God, saying:

"Sovereign Lord, as you have promised, you may now dismiss your servant in peace. For my eyes have seen your salvation, which you have prepared in the sight of all people: A light for revelation to the Gentiles, and for glory to your people Israel."

The child's father and mother marvelled at what was said about him. Then Simeon blessed them and said to Mary, his mother: "This child is destined to cause the falling and rising of many in Israel, and to be a sign that will be spoken against, so that the thoughts of many hearts will be revealed. And a sword will pierce your own soul too."

Simeon

I've been waiting
With expectant joy
For the promised one;
The rescuer,
Sent from God
To set his people free.

When I see him,
I will be ready to depart this life in peace.

I've been longing
With expectant hope
For the promised one;
The Messiah,
Sent from God to make all things new.

When I see him,
I will be ready to depart this life in peace.

Today I am rejoicing
With indescribable gladness.
He has come!
Our Saviour;
A light to reveal God
To the nations.
Salvation is here.

Now that I have seen him
I am ready to depart this life in peace.

Only when you've met him
Will you be able to say the same.

John 3:16-17

"For God so loved the world, that he gave his one and only Son, that whoever believes in him should not perish but have eternal life. For God did not send his Son into the world to condemn the world, but to save the world through him."

1 Peter 3:18a

"For Christ died for sins once for all, the righteous for the unrighteous, to bring you to God."

1 Corinthians 15:3–4

"For what I received I passed on to you as of first importance: That Christ died for our sins according to the Scriptures, that he was buried, that he was raised on the third day according to the Scriptures."

Not just an ordinary baby

A long journey,
No room at the inn,
A dusty stable,
A newborn King
Lying in a manger.
Not just an ordinary baby.

Shepherds watch,
Angels sing.
Guiding star,
Wise men bring
their gifts from far away.
Not just an ordinary baby.

Wind is stilled,
Dead are raised,
Lepers healed,
Crowds amazed
at what they see.
Not just an ordinary baby.

Totally innocent,
Taking my blame,
Nails, thorns
Agonizing pain
upon a cross.
Not just an ordinary baby.

Three days later,
Tomb open wide.
Grave clothes folded,
He's alive
And lives forever!
Not just an ordinary baby.

Death defeated
Victory won
Trust in Jesus
Sins are gone
And forgotten.
Not just an ordinary baby.

Earthly strength
Future glory
Jesus loves me
Amazing story!
Not just an ordinary baby.

Loved

Loved with an amazing love:
A love that brought the King of Heaven to earth;
Born a helpless baby in a dusty stable.

Loved with a sacrificial love:
A love that sent the sinless Son of God to die upon a cross
For my sin and yours.

Loved with an unconditional love:
A love that does not depend on beauty or intelligence;
A love that accepts me just as I am.

Loved with an unchanging love:
A love that does not decrease with failure or increase with success;
A love that doesn't fade with age or frailty.

Loved with an everlasting love:
Love that spans beyond human comprehension;
Love that will sustain me throughout my days on earth and into eternity.

Romans 3:23

"For all have sinned and fall short of the glory of God."

Romans 5:8

"But God demonstrates his own love for us in this: While we were still sinners, Christ died for us."

Romans 10:13

"Everyone who calls on the name of the Lord will be saved."

A Heavenly Plan

From heaven's glory to a borrowed stable;
From robes of splendour to swaddling clothes.
God became man;
A heavenly plan
To bring God's children home.

From heaven's glory to a wooden cross;
Taking my punishment, bearing my pain.
God crucified;
The sinless one died
To bring God's children home.

From heaven's glory to a borrowed tomb;
But death could not hold the King.
He arose from the grave;
He is mighty to save
And bring God's children home.

From heaven's glory he will one day return
To receive all those who trust him as their Lord.
Fulfilling a plan;
A heavenly plan
To bring God's children home.

John 14:6

"Jesus answered, 'I am the way, and the truth, and the life. No one comes to the Father except through me.' "

Acts 4:12

"Salvation is found in no one else, for there is no other name under heaven given to men by which we must be saved."

Jesus my Lord

Baby of Bethlehem;
Born in a cattle shed,
Revealed to humble men,
Jesus my Lord.

Jesus of Galilee;
Reaching to those in need,
Fully God, fully man,
Jesus my Lord.

Saviour of Calvary;
Sinless yet crucified,
Paying the debt I owe,
Jesus my Lord.

Open tomb, empty grave;
Risen again.
Death, our final enemy, defeated
By Jesus my Lord.

One day he'll come again,
And take home with him to reign,
Those who have trusted him and known
Jesus as Lord.

Light in my darkness,
Strength in my weakness,
Hope when all hope seems gone,
Jesus my Lord.

Love unconditional,
Mercy unimaginable,
Grace beyond measure,
Jesus my Lord.

Romans 6:23

"For the wages of sin is death, but the gift of God is eternal life in Christ Jesus our Lord."

Ephesians 2: 8-9

"For it is by grace you have been saved, through faith—and this not from yourselves, it is the gift of God— not by works, so that no one can boast."

Gifts

Christmas gifts come in all shapes and sizes:
Big gifts, small gifts,
desired gifts and unwanted gifts.
Exciting gifts and practical gifts
(like socks - again!).

**The best gift of all
was wrapped in swaddling clothes
and laid in a manger.
The precious Son of God
became human
for us.**

Christmas gifts come in all shapes and sizes:
Big gifts, small gifts,
desired gifts and unwanted gifts.
Exciting gifts and practical gifts
(like socks - again!).

**The best gift of all
was nailed to a wooden cross
and died in my place.
The precious Son of God
took sin's punishment
for us.**

Christmas gifts come in all shapes and sizes:
Big gifts, small gifts,
desired gifts and unwanted gifts.

Exciting gifts and practical gifts
(like socks - again!).

The best gift of all
was buried in a borrowed tomb
but the grave could not hold him.
The precious Son of God
rose from the dead
and defeated the final enemy
for us.

Christmas gifts come in all shapes and sizes:
Big gifts, small gifts,
desired gifts and unwanted gifts.
Exciting gifts and practical gifts
(like socks - again!).

The best gift of all
ascended into heaven
to prepare a place for those
who have trusted him as LORD.
Jesus the precious Son of God
will one day return
to judge the earth
and take his children home.

Christmas gifts come in all shapes and sizes:
Big gifts, small gifts,
desired gifts and unwanted gifts.
Exciting gifts and practical gifts
(like socks - again!).

Jesus, the precious Son of God;
Will he be your greatest gift this Christmas?

Jesus, you're wonderful

Jesus you're wonderful;
We celebrate your birth.
You gave up heaven's glory
to dwell here on this earth.
Son of God, Immanuel- God with us,
I give my life to you

Jesus you're wonderful;
The King high over all.
You heal the broken-hearted,
and comfort those who fall.
Jesus, healer, Saviour, Lord and friend,
I give my life to you.

Jesus you're wonderful;
You love me as I am.
I cannot face this world alone,
but with your strength I can.
You're the rock, on which I stand secure,
I give my life to you.

Jesus you're wonderful;
You paid the debt I owed.
You suffered death upon a cross
to bring me back to God.
Greater love has no man shown than this:
You gave your life for me.

Jesus you're wonderful;
I wait for your return,
when you will come to judge the earth
and take your children home.
Then in heaven we will reign with you
for all eternity.

John 14:1-3

"Do not let your hearts be troubled. Trust in God; trust also in me. In my Father's house are many rooms; if it were not so, I would have told you. I am going there to prepare a place for you. And if I go and prepare a place for you, I will come back and take you to be with me that you also may be where I am."

My King

A King stepped from his throne room
and became a child like me;
He gave up heaven's splendour
for earth's humanity.

He came to earth as one of us;
A Saviour, born to die.
Perfect God and perfect man
on a cross, lifted high.

If his story ended there,
my hope would be in vain;
I'd still be lost,
I'd still be dying
in my sin and shame.

He died for me upon that cross,
my guilty soul to save.
But praise his name, my LORD arose
and triumphed over the grave.

He died my death,
He bore my shame
because he loved me so.
My heart was black with
sin's dark stain;

He washed me
white as snow.

One day when Jesus comes or calls
I'll see my Saviour's face;
Forever I will worship him
in that holy place.

What will you do?

The presents have been opened,
The carols have been sung,
And the shops are already making room
for their new displays
of Easter Eggs.

What will you do with Jesus?
Will you crown him as Lord of your life
or put him back in the box for another year?

Christmas dinner has been eaten,
The visitors have gone,
The last cracker has been pulled
and we are all facing
turkey sandwiches
for the next fortnight.

What will you do with Jesus?
Will you crown him as Lord of your life
or put him back in the box for another year?

The decorations are disappearing,
The fairy lights have been switched off,
And a new year is looming
with resolutions to be made
....and broken.

What will you do with Jesus?
Will you crown him as Lord of your life
or put him back in the box for another year?

A Christmas Blessing

This Christmas,

May you experience the excitement of the shepherds as they hurried to Bethlehem; the wonder of the Wise Men as they gazed at the promised King; and the peace proclaimed in the song of the angels.

May the lights remind you of the Light of the World who has come to defeat darkness forever.

May each gift remind you of Jesus, the greatest gift of all.

Perhaps, this Christmas, there is an empty chair at your table and everything going on around you is a stark reminder of how things used to be. May you know the love and comfort of a Saviour who knows what it feels like to weep at the grave of a loved one; a Saviour who came to defeat death forever and who brings hope in even the most difficult of situations.

Whatever circumstances you find yourself in, may you know the love of God who loved you enough to send his only son to die for you. May you know the true peace and joy that only he can bring.

Amen

Conclusion

Let's return to the verse that we looked at in the opening pages of this booklet:

John 3:16

"For God so loved the world that he gave his one and only Son, that whoever believes in him shall not perish but have eternal life."

Have you ever tried to put your own name into that verse?

For God so loved _______________ that he gave his one and only son that (if) _____________________ believes in him, ____________________ shall not perish but have eternal life.

God made you. He loves you and he wants to have a personal relationship with you, but no matter how good or bad you think you are, you have a problem – sin. God is pure and holy and therefore this sin separates you from him; it stops you from having a personal relationship with God and it means that you cannot be with him in heaven - God's perfect home.

God is a God of justice and therefore sin must be punished. The punishment for sin is death – separation from God forever in a place the Bible calls hell.

However, God is also a God of love. God loves you so much that he sent his only son, Jesus, into the world. He was born as a baby in Bethlehem; he grew up and lived a pure, spotless life. He never sinned, yet he was put to death on a cross to take the punishment that YOUR sin deserved. He died to pay the penalty for your sin and mine so that we wouldn't have to. What amazing love!

Three days later, Jesus rose from the dead, showing that he has the power to defeat death! Forty days later he ascended into heaven where he lives today to prepare a place for all who have trusted in him to forgive their sin. He will one day return to judge the earth and take all of those who have trusted in him to be with him in heaven forever.

Jesus is the only answer to the problem of sin. If you want to have a personal relationship with God and go to heaven someday, your sins must be forgiven. You can't do it on your own, no matter how hard you try.

If you believe that Jesus died for you and ask him to forgive you for rejecting God's rule over you and choosing to go your own way, he will! Then, when God looks at you, he will not treat you as your sin deserves. He will treat you as pure and spotless- just like Jesus!

Trusting in Jesus isn't easy. It doesn't mean that all your problems will disappear and it doesn't mean that you won't sin any more – you will, no matter how hard you try, but God has promised never to leave you and to help you every day to become more like Jesus!

One day, you will meet God, either when you die or when Jesus returns. When you meet God, what will he say? Will you be welcomed into his presence for all eternity because you have accepted his amazing gift and trusted in Jesus to forgive you for your sins? Or will you be separated from him forever because you rejected his amazing gift and tried to do it on your own? The Bible tells us that nobody knows when Jesus will return to earth. If you met God today, would you be ready?

These three simple steps explain how you can know Jesus as your own Saviour.

A: Accept that you are a sinner and that you need to have your sins forgiven. You must be sorry for all the wrong things you have done and desire to go God's way.

B: Believe that Jesus, the Son of God, died for you on the cross, taking the punishment for your sin and rose from the grave to bring you to God.

C: Confess, in prayer, that you want Jesus to be the Lord of your life and that you want to live your life for him. Trust him to be your Saviour.

There are no magic words or formulae; just come to Jesus as you are. If you want to trust in Jesus as your own saviour, but are struggling to know how to begin, the following prayer may help you.

Dear God,

I know that I am a sinner and I need your forgiveness. Thank you for loving me enough to send your son, Jesus Christ, into the world to die for me on a cross, taking the punishment that my sin deserved. I believe that he rose from the dead and lives today in heaven, preparing a place for all of those who have trusted in him. I am sorry for all the times that I have disobeyed you. I want to turn away from my sin but I know that I can't do this alone – please help me to turn away from my sin and become more like Jesus. I thank you that you have promised that you will always be with me and that you will never let me go. I believe in you, I love you and I want to live for you from this day on.

Amen.

If you have prayed this or a similar prayer, or if you have any questions or comments about what you have read, please contact *three16@live.com*

It would be great to hear from you. No question will be considered unimportant or insignificant!

Alternatively, you can contact the person who gave you this booklet at: